Out of the Welter

Poems by
Arthur Madson

FIREWEED PRESS

Out of the Welter

Copyright © 2009 by Marianne Madson

Published by Fireweed Press, Madison, Wisconsin,
in the United States of America.
Printed by Inkwell Printers, Dodgeville, Wisconsin;
pre-press work by Deena Vinger. All rights reserved.

ACKNOWLEDGEMENTS

Thanks to the following publications in which versions of some of these poems appeared:

"Monet's Haystacks," "Sunbathe," and "Unendowed Chair" appeared in *Good Manure*, copyright 1998 by Art Madson.

"Class of '44," "Elbows and Onions," "Even in Dreams," "How to Grow Young Painting Pictures," "Interstate," "Sweet Sixteen" [as ". . .and Never Been Kissed"] and "Taking in the Wash" appeared in *Blue-Eyed Boy*, copyright 1993 by Arthur Madson.

"A Bend in the River," "Elevator," and "Silk Purse" appeared in *Plastering the Cracks*, copyright 1993 by Arthur Madson.

"Bullheads," "Let Me Call You Sweetheart," "Of Lines," "Out of the Welter," "St. Patrick's Day in Dane County," appeared in *Coming Up Sequined*, copyright 1991 by Arthur Madson.

Special thanks to Robin Chapman, Jeri McCormick, and Richard Roe for their work in compiling this posthumous collection with the help of Marianne Madson. Thanks, also, to the participants in Arthur's manuscript group.

Cover design by Amy Kittleson
Cover photograph by Joseph Justus, Arthur's grandson

ISBN 1-878660-23-3
978-1-878660-23-7

For Marianne

Contents

Vines Heavy with Promise

Cousins		10
I	three dozens of cousins	
II	like triplets, almost	
III	leaf-extended tables	
IV	teetering with care	
V	examples . . . or exceptions	
VI	relativity	
VII	had familiar names	
VIII	no one came really back	
IX	singularity	
X	cozenage	

Even in Dreams	16
Elevator	17
Of Lines	18
Pickles & Pie	19
Winging	20
To a College Girl, Fifty Years Later	22
Out of the Welter	23
Interstate	24
Mending Harness	25
Hands Like Wings	26
Taking in the Wash	27
Redwings Rasp	28
Let Me Call You Sweetheart	29
A Bend in the River	30
St. Patrick's Day in Dane County	31
Quite Contrary	32
Class of '44	33
Sweet Sixteen	34
Silk Purse	35
Left Hand	36
Bullheads	37
Halloween	38
Cops and Robbers	40
Sunbathe	41
How to Grow Young Painting Pictures	42

Reconstruct the Harmonies

Milk and Honey	44
Because It's There	45
Purple Cow	46
Volunteers	48
Last Words	50
Forecast	51
Gravity	52
Genevieve Walrath Madson, 1896-1949	53
Genealogy	54
Unendowed Chair	55
Genealogist	56
Portrait	57
Elbows and Onions	58
Tomatoes Are Ripe, Are Ripe	59
Sumac	60
Taking Off	61
Somatic	62
Snow	63
The Next Degree	64
Monet's Haystacks	65
Invocation	66
Witching the Night	67
White Wine	68
Closets	69
The Man Who Lived Among the Cannibals	70
Visitation	71
Intensive Care	72
Facing Forward	73
Golden Year	74
Assent, and Bright Lights	75
After Shock	76
After the Bypass	77
Evening at Home	78
Trumpet	79

Vines Heavy with Promise

*two glasses of vin rosé
remind me of summer grapes
and vines heavy with promise,
inform these lines I think and pen*

Halloween

Cousins

I
"three dozens of cousins"

I grew up with cousins,
older cousins, younger cousins, same-age cousins,
boy cousins, girl cousins,
blonde cousins, brunette cousins,
town cousins, farm cousins,
brown-eyed cousins, blue-eyed cousins,
even a green-eyed, red-haired cousin,
two fat cousins, fair cousins, tanned cousins,
freckled, pimpled, peach-skinned cousins,
athletic cousins, cheering cousins, clumsy cousins,
one crippled-from-infantile-paralysis cousin,
bike-owning cousins, bike-borrowing cousins,
Lutheran cousins, some Methodist cousins,
Madson cousins, and other cousins,
three dozens of cousins.
I grew up with cousins;
thought everyone did.

II
"like triplets, almost"

I grew up in the same small town
my father did;
his older brother and younger sister
lived there too,
and thirteen kids, thirteen cousins,
allies always and at home
in all three houses.
Two cousins and I, one boy, one girl,
one blonde, one brown, one Madson, one other,
like triplets, almost,
went through six grades together,
went to Sunday School together,
played kick-the-can, anny-I-over,
jacks and hopscotch and hide-and-seek,
marbles and mumbledy-peg, together,
jumped rope, together,
roller skated, sledded, giggled, teased, fought,
and partied, together.

III
"leaf-extended tables"

All the cousins grew up on farms
or small towns
and didn't live far away—
hardly a Sunday went by
we didn't load up and visit
one of the relatives,
or an aunt and uncle and cousins
came to visit us.
All of the uncles were fishermen,
and were given to tales
and talk of politics, and hard times;
none a drunk, but all moderate consumers of beer,
and great Sunday feasters
at summer picnics in the park or on the lawn,
at winter dinners of meat loaf,
with homemade chili sauce,
muffins and butter, real butter,
creamed cauliflower, carrots,
home-crocked sauerkraut and baked potatoes,
or roast pork and mashed potatoes with pork gravy,
spiced whole peaches, cottage cheese,
apple pie à la mode,
and for the adults and older cousins,
cups and cups of coffee
at leaf-extended tables.

IV
"teetering with care"

Younger cousins at card tables tangled feet,
bumped elbows, made faces, grabbed
and gabbed and ate only what
and as little or much as we chose,
free from adults as long as we got along,
and so we did, teetering with care
on the edge.
The older among us
enjoyed our rank, pseudo adults,
and grieved and hankered for
graduation from Kool-Aid and wiggly table
to coffee and grown-up dining.

V
"examples . . . or exceptions"

Parents and aunts and uncles often spoke
of their cousins,
and of the children of those cousins,
cousins once removed, our second cousins.
Mom had a set of nine double cousins,
all with children.
We all knew the degrees of relationship,
and adults spoke darkly of first cousins
marrying,
warning of genetic danger,
pointing at cousins who had married anyway,
hinting of passion, rebellion, Eden's apple,
and whose children all, sure enough,
paid the price—
examples, every one,
or exceptions that proved the rule.

VI
"relativity"

All we cousins gossiped of our other cousins,
cousins on the other side,
unrelated cousins complicating
relativity,
yet when we sometimes met these cousins,
visits overlapping,
we felt an instant twinge
of cousinhood.
In the family trees we climbed and combed,
we'd find cousins twice or more removed,
and cousins of third degree, or fourth,
so that sometimes, citing Genesis,
we claimed
all the world as cousins.

VII
"had familiar names"

Each family, Mom's and Dad's,
gathered for a family picnic
every June and August—

sacred family holidays.
All the aunts and uncles and the cousins
always came, even the Catholic ones,
skipping Mass that Sunday,
and always a family or two
of some second cousins we'd never seen before,
or only once, long ago, but knew from family talk—
and always they turned out to be
blonde, brown, stingy, free,
formal, casual, stuck-up, friendly,
just like all the first cousins,
and had familiar names.

Cousins chose up sides for volleyball
or softball, remembering one another's skills,
jumped rope, pitched horseshoes,
played 'Old Maid,' 'Authors,' 'Eights are Wild,'
and talked and walked and flirted—
one can have an awful crush
on a slightly older cousin—
and ate.
Fried chicken, ham, fish—
pickerels, bullheads, croppies, perch—
pans and pans of baked beans,
Waldorf salad, potato salads, tossed salads,
Deviled eggs, homemade breads, jams and jellies
and honey, sweet corn, cucumbers,
creamed new potatoes parsley-sprigged,
sliced tomatoes and iced tea,
pies and cakes and red, ripe melons—
oh, the spitting of seeds—
every June I stuffed myself
on the olives my mom's sister brought.

VIII
"no one came really back"

That was years and years ago,
more than I care to count,
growing up before the war,
and I haven't kept up
with the cousins;
we've scattered from Virginia
to California.

My sister stays in touch,
and her letters to me include
a chorus of news of cousins.

"Della's Eileen had her first,
Della and Harold's fourth grandchild;
Jerry retired in June,
and he and Nancy moved to Arizona.
They found a cancer, Thank God, in time,
in Myrna, she had a breast removed"—
which one, I wonder, seeing a slim, blonde,
teen-aged girl in a red swimsuit—
"poor Ralph, laid off last spring
and now his pension sliced,
Karen's still working
at Mrs. Paul's, she's on the line,
hopes she can hang on two more years
till Social Security."
Cousins' children seem to graduate
by the dozen,
and marry and re-marry,
change jobs, move about,
give birth, get sick and well, constantly.
Each item I'm grateful for,
whether news be good or bad;
most start a flow of memories
of early times, static times,
lilac times—
times lost, times over,
sauce for reverie
preserved in clumsy photo albums.

The war scattered the cousins,
killed one, shot up another,
but we all left, even those who stayed behind,
left our cousin times,
and the years after
were no return;
no one came really back.
The post-war years, getting-started years,
catch-up years,
were years of losing track.

IX
"singularity"

My children barely know their cousins,
let alone mine,
have grown up deprived
of cousins,
though, never having known,
see nothing amiss
in our family's
singularity,
and think me odd
when I reminisce—
"That's Dad."
My children barely know their cousins,
don't attend their weddings,
nor the funerals
of my aunts and uncles,
though I do,
memories winding down,
mostly done;

X
"cozenage"

and though there's always smiles and hugs
and cousins' kissing,
there's not much to say;
ghosts from family picnics,
younger selves, crowding the pews,
drooping their heads,
dropping their purple sprigs,
telling over and over,
loss, loss.

I grew up with cozenage;
every grown-up does.

Even in Dreams

Flower in a garden world
and I, a gust-borne bee
blown in, a refugee
from clover fields contested for
where swashbucklers are preferred
and "peace" is a newspeak word

and falling in love
with the freshest nectar
in the bluest bloom
falling in love
with a garden world
with adventure undone.

Wedding in haste without a priest
nor chapel in the garden
and she loved me
whoever I was
and I loved her
who never was

but her ear was caught
by the whistling thrush
my eye by the stooping hawk—
in turn we bit
the fatal fruit—
she sang, I wrote.

Even in dreams of she-and-I
of pastoral love
and Paradise garden
the plot ripens, autumn happens
and squirrels the ending
awry.

Elevator

We boys swarmed up the iron rungs
parked on the siding
and raced along the tops
jumping from car to car—
robbers boarding the swaying train.

Looting the passengers,
rifling the baggage car,
we jumped to the shed roof,
spurred up the foothill shingles
and along the ridge top
to the sheet-metal mountain, abutting,
hid the horses, and scaled the drainpipes,
foxing the posse.

> My nephew and his friends,
> with permissions and technology
> unavailable to us, all those years ago,
> ride to the top of the same peak
> on the metal mountain's electricity,
> step freely off into nothing,
> and rappel down the cliff
> in great bouncing loops.

Reading journal poems,
I still inch up that mountain side,
the poets go inside the elevator,
whizz to the top,
step freely off,
and float, descend,
run back up,
spiders on the threads they've spun
from their own essence.

Leaning way out from the drainpipe,
arching my back,
I can see the spiders, sometimes,
jiggling on the end of their lines,
anchoring,
if the sun and haze are just right,
a filament
of rainbow.

17

Of Lines

Say I'm writing lines,
paddling along, snug and trim,
shipping a little water around a bend,
and the bottom falls out—
rapids.
That's when I know.
You taste the spray,
feel the rocks,
sit on your heart—
but you need still waters
and a steady beat
to made landfall.

Take this afternoon.
I'm walking across campus
past that knot of dark marigolds
and the taller spikes of fragrant stocks
they're banked against—
a hot, arid oasis
in this green August desert,
and swinging by
a college girl in summer shorts
lilts a greeting—
oh, blue water and date palms,
hours in the afternoon.
Rapids.
And, with a little steering,
keeping of balance, three or four
guiding strokes—poetry.

Or remember those times,
we're sitting around in the evening,
nothing special on TV,
postponed books at our elbows,
we talk a bit, debate a drink,
and all at once you're looking
an invitation. Seconds split;
it's free-fall time.
Rapids.
And then we rise, and read.
Still waters
to revise in.

Pickles & Pie

A hard-headed friend of mine
grows glib cucumbers
brines slices of life
jars them with alum
store-bought dill and mustard-seed
and brings his pickled take
to every party gathering
Valentine's to New Year's.

Meanwhile I prune and mulch
canebrake berries
pick and freeze
bleed from thorns
all summer long
and bring a deep-dish berry pie
to every party gathering
Valentine's to New Year's.

Dill chips garnish every plate
crinkled, colored, crisp
enlivening the party.
My crusts aren't ironic,
my fillings look too sugared
set teeth on edge
and my shells come home untested
my metaphors untasted.

Winging

It's the twenties. Coolidge prosperity,
silk undershirts, bootleg booze,
football, college, work.
Model-T, paved roads, birds and bees,
squeeze, spank, squawl,
crib and blanket life.

Snow flies, sore feet,
impetigo, a diamond necklace
round wrinkled neck,
the smell of newsprint
and popcorn, Sunday paper
on Saturday night, Miss Ross
saying "Read. Learn to read."

Write. Are you writing?
Love poems. The high-school girl
loved them. Eyes, lips, teeth,
tongue. You are lucky.
Heavy breathing. All the clichés
alive and true.

One day it's war; you wonder what
the papers wrote in peace-time.
GI years, march and class,
the eagle shits, and then it doesn't.
Your fly-wings are twisted off;
crawl off to Oklahoma,
elude the horned toads,
spin a cocoon, read, study,
produce term papers.

Cogitate. Dissertate.
Sleep. Transform. Grow
thorax, tentacles, new wings, feet.
Reproductive cells. Ingest
experience. Numbs the pain.
Correct student writing.
Fall in love with Shakespeare.

Emerge. The soft-voiced actor
is now president, pyramids
public debt, trickles down
prosperity, is re-elected.
You're in flannels now,
retired, writing, your own books.

Dipping into the culture
dish, tubing nectar,
flitting here, there,
scenting soul mates
ten miles up wind,
a long road, and blue bruises,
green chomp to sweet pheromone.

To a College Girl, Fifty Years Later

When you re-visit me
and our eyes touch,
like polish cloth
on old silver,

and the remembered taste
of you catches me,
like hands spanning
a slim waist,

when I stare, stumbling,
down long afternoons,
and outside the windows
bare-limbed trees
bend, like us,
I tell myself
there was a spring.

I hear the May murmur
of two voices never at a loss
for things to say, words ceasing only
for more intense communication,

I see the years strip away,
see hair re-blonde, feet dance,
mouth red velvet yes I promise
I see
that college boy

mirrored
in your eyes.

Out of the Welter

Braising our innards
in the sun glancing
off the water, off the sand,
we foil the beams, wrapped in lotion,
remain unbrowned, bathers as intrepid
as those in the water.
We stretch our toes
to meet the wave, dive through,
and come up sequined.

To be in love,
on a beach like this
is easy as breathing under water
through a snorkel tube—
impossible not to,
once you've learned how.

To make love,
after a day like this,
to connect the dots
while the ocean exhales,
a block away,
while the sun broils
a night away,
is impossible,
once you've learned how
not to.

Interstate

A whole hot day of listening
to the the gray topsoil disappear
from between the corn rows
as I drive across Indiana,
Illinois, and into Iowa.
I'd like to stop and study
the bull thistles, their spicules
so fierce they're permitted to seed.
I would like to understand
the stare of crouching crows
feeding on carrion.
I would like to think highway clover leaves,
spreading in fours, are lucky.

I sometimes tell my father,
resting in his plot for forty years,
of modern farming methods—
of lawns, asphalt driveways,
long ranch houses, and double,
triple garages, solving the topsoil problem;
of grazing junked autos fenced away from
the Holsteins and Spotted Poland Chinas;
of gaunt windmills in the middle of fields,
their wheels and vanes gone,
of gnarled tractors, discs, spreaders,
rooted in pasture corners
where once field stones grew—
and perhaps my voice is still enough,
small enough,
that he hears.

Mending Harness

Sun glinting off the ice dagger,
and I remember the icicle that formed
every winter, sparkling off the eave
over the kitchen window. I see Dad
coming in from the stable, leather harness
hanging on his arm and shoulder. Seeing me,
he would trot, whinny, and drape the leather
on my thin shoulders. I staggered
under that burden, and thought of the horses
wearing that weight effortlessly all day
in the field, as Dad removed
his outdoor wraps, then the harness,
to be spread on a couple of kitchen chairs.
Like a team plodding up and down corn rows
under a summer sun, so Dad worked,
next to the kitchen range, winter chore
of mending harness.

The smell of leather and of horse,
and something else, dried sweat,
I presume now, and horse stall—
hay, stray, manure, took over
the kitchen, mixing with the coffee,
six or seven cups, steaming, black,
that Dad consumed, and he told me
between sips, between straps
and snaps and rivets,
about the first job he'd had,
off the farm: stable boy
in the Albert Lea Fire Station,
and of how the horses braced themselves,
when the alarm sounded,
(this years before Pavlov and his dog)
to receive the shock of the harness,
suspended above them, rigged to fall
on their backs when the lever was pulled.

Still today, sitting in my retirement kitchen
drinking coffee and the fire truck wails past,
still today, driving between cities passing
working farms and men on tractors, I feel
that heavy harness settling on my shoulders,
smell that other kitchen, till the crops
Dad planted, sixty years ago.

Hands Like Wings

I dozed off
this drowsy August afternoon
reclining on the patio
reading in today's Poetry Review
of the poet looking at his hands
and surprised to see his father's hands
his father's carpenter's hands
appended to the poet-professor's mind.

I did not dream of my father
nor of hands.
My hands are not like his—
what used to be called horn-handed
farmer's hands molded by the tractor wheel
by tool handles, cows' teats
barbed-wire scars in the palms
from vaulting the pasture fence once
being chased by the bull.
My hands are small and smooth
though strong enough in handshakes
having tractored, milked, and handled tools
once upon a time.

I rejoin the wakeful present
to a monarch throned on my pants leg
its wings folded
like hands in prayer
its butterfly hands
just like its father's.
Soon it will be off to Mexico.
We sit still, resting
before winging across the Gulf.

Taking in the Wash

The evening empties
the double row of pines
of their silence and green shadows,
the barn of its red recesses,
the yard and pasture
of their pools of sunlight.

Clemmie's taking in the wash.
The clothes-pinned legs and waists
and chests, alive on the line,
lie limp as noodles
in the basket.

The calico cat
measuring the lessening light
in her pupils,
prowls toward the fields,
pauses at the basket
for a rub against ankles,
for a caress behind her ears.

The sky closes,
freeing two owls to hoot
from the grove behind the barn.
Clemmie stops in the garden,
picks a handful of mums,
straightens,
and crushes them to her nose,
the whole of evening
in her gesture.

Redwings Rasp

Walking the road I used to walk
sixty years, five hundred miles ago,
I gauge the gravel and ruts
with hind-foresight, walking backwards
into the future. Cross-tied utility poles
blaze the way, and I step along, breathing
the stinking shrinkage of spring freshness
in the roadside march, the ripe brownness
of tomorrow's corn, the refreshing pull
of journey's end.

Cottonwoods shimmer up ahead, silver
in a breeze that doesn't reach this low,
and beyond are peaks this prairie never grew
and gullies to cross, a sky to climb.
Brushing away pestering gnats,
shrinking from the splatter of passing cars,
wiping my eyes in the yellow dust,
I march past barking dogs, working farmsteads,
stepping to the drumming of the utility wires,
their beat and loops metering light and words.

There is a power in repeating
a May or June journey, mending
the fallen arches and torn memories.
The poles still thrust toward the fluff
of clouds, and have to be tied down,
their zinging wires forecasting the past,
re-telling tomorrow. Redwings rasp and dive-bomb,
stones test the pitching arm. The westering sun
prettifies the sky and all below,
and promises to hang above the horizon
as long as I keep my feet.

Let Me Call You Sweetheart

Under a summer sun
mid tall and headed grass
in the country schoolyard
nobody had mowed since May
Linda Beth and I
picked wild roses,
a fruit jar full
for our mothers, we said
but not really,
and the clanging cowbell
was violins.

I pricked my finger
and Linda Beth said
"Let me kiss it
and make it well."
The green corn stretched and grew,
the violins played,
Linda's hands lifted
my stricken finger,
her lips jounced my heart.
We dawdled in the swings
and the chains sang.

Many kisses have come and gone
roses bloomed, and violins played.
Grass has headed,
Linda Beth moved away
the next year, or was it the next—
anyway, it was Johnny Loken
she wrote to—but a pricked finger
still transports me
to that wild-rose summer
but nowadays I ask the wound
be cross-hatched, and sucked.

A Bend in the River

I am tired of canned carols
and streams of shoppers
and the bundle that's my overcoat
here on the bench beside me,
tired of the controlled weather,
of the fan-tailed goldfish
yellowing the hours
in their coin-lined pool.
Fish! I would be back in Canada
on lakes as smooth and blue
as on the map, my prow ripping
across pristine inlets,
like tearing an old sheet for rags,
and coming home to Clemmie
with a tub of walleyes
and ghosts to lay.

Fish! A miracle! A laughing
young woman has kicked off
her shoes and is wading
in the pool, her skirt gathered
nearly to her crotch,
scrabbling among the dimes
and pennies and goldfish
with her toes, and now
it's forty years ago,
I'm already in the river
and Clemmie's wading toward me,
giving her legs, those marvelous legs,
to the dark water.
It's June,
and the moon's
in the first quarter.

St. Patrick's Day in Dane County

The house this evening smells of melt,
crocus, and raw, fresh earth—
you aired all afternoon.
And here you sit, all green
for St. Pat, basking
in the absence of snakes.
The schedule calls for summer solstice
or St. John's Day—thereabouts.

I watch your tan embroidery hoop,
round against your woman's shape,
revolve the six-sided pencil
in my hand—how do you keep
unthimbled fingers safe?
("By the pricking of my thumbs,
something evil this way comes.")
Oh, saint, not witch, guide my thought.

Outside, an owl hoots
and in my mind I see
a skittering rabbit, a swoop,
and awful talons grip—
hear the stricken squeak
("to fetch a rabbit skin
to wrap my baby bunting in.")
Oh, St. John, protect the meek.

We've let the clocks run down,
turned the TV on,
put dinner in the oven,
set the wine to breathe—
you stitch, I watch,
you knot, I rhyme—
St. John, St. Pat, you'll tell us
when it's time.

Quite Contrary

Bachelor's Degree
of legal age
old married woman
three weeks now—
still, their student housing
staggered her—
a plexus blow.

Row on row
of anchored, mobile homes
shell-shocked veterans
sitting under
bent box elder trees.

Ice man and box
and draining pan
floor so cold, come winter
box and man retired.
Oven a warped tin box
to set on the burner—
a perfect excuse for her
bride's meringue—
but her tears flowed
just the same.

Communal bathroom
shower room with eight faucets
grinning from the wall.
Coming home
from *Moulin Rouge*
and chancing upon
eight pregnant soapers
eight parallel parentheses
lathering in unison
she had a migraine
six nights in a row.

But after a year
of smoothing the wrinkles
and typing his thesis
she knew that she
had mastered the course
but only he
got the Degree.

Class of '44

I sat beside blonde Arlene
in senior English class,
thanking the accident of alphabet,
trying to entwine her L and my M.

Sitting beside "Daisy Mae"
and telling her jokes
from the Saturday night shows
she never stayed home to hear,
I tasted her eyes, her lips,
her breath, teeth, tongue
as she laughed.

At the class reunion in May
blonde Daisy won the prize
for having come the longest distance,
and when the class "Ambitions"
(oh, high school foolishness)
were read and hers came out
"Professional Necker,"
a blush spread
on those still smooth cheeks
under the frost-white hair,
and the guys at the head table
looked wise-guy looks.

Sitting beside Daisy Mae
after the dinner and speeches,
the V of her now name
a new gap to bridge,
I tasted again her eyes, lips,
breath, teeth, tongue,
as she reminisced.

"I'll never forget, Art,
your bulletin-board notice—
'Lost: GOLDEN MOMENTS. Art Madson.'"
and as she laughed I was content
to let the others swig
the cheap wine of youth—
I was rolling on my tongue
an aged and piquant bouquet.

Sweet Sixteen

Barely dawn, December morning,
and walking my trap line
along the frozen drainage ditch
dividing corn field from pasture,
just sixteen and counting the first skins
in advance . . .

I found a skunk, alive,
and put a .22 slug
in its head,
then another skunk,
a coon drowned (which Dad had predicted)
where an open tile bubbled into the ditch,
and a weasel, dodging, snapping, defying me,
hard to shoot.

A dozen traps, four pelts, an hour,
and my bank account was swelling.
In the last trap
a coon's paw,
the leg gnawed through
just above the steel jaws.
My money dwindled,
and I hated the animal
for swindling me of its skin.

Silk Purse

See piggy eyes
curly tail
prehensile snout
in your breakfast bacon.
See the hanging, flayed carcass
guts, blood, brains removed.
Underfoot,
pink sawdust sweepings.

See the unringed nose
plowing the pasture
divining
succulent grubs
and fat roots
forecasting
prime link sausages.

See the hungry
nursing sow
with her learning litter
nosing through cow droppings
oinking over
kernels flavored through
four stomachs
olfactory cud
and glutinous sty.

See her nap
in her drinking trough,
wallow in mud
grow sleekly fat
larding her pen.
Behind the Christmas crown roast
the Easter ham, the family feast
see piggy eyes
curly tail
hear the oink,
taste the swill.

Left Hand

You squeeze under the log, the rock,
see a familiar in the line
where perpendiculars meet,
coil in the dust,
wait, mesmerize—

strike with your hollow fang,
turn your meal around,
unhinge your jaw, and swallow,
squeak first,
alive.

When you travel you go
earthbound, crawling, grass
a spiky forest, molehills alps.
You go around, under, pry into,
sidle, slide.

Every man's hand against you,
you spearing every heel,
you gloat in being the enemy, the other,
soar into the stars,
Ophiuchus, Serpens.

In the black hole you lurk,
nothing escaping you,
not even gravity,
hewing a corner of hell
in the heavens.

Bullheads

We boys used to take our willow-branch poles,
our can of earthworms, our straight-rigged lines,
lead sinkers and corks to mis-named Crystal Lake,
and almost always caught what we were after—
the bobbing of the cork as the fish nibbled
or nosed the worm, and the wonder,

would it bite, would it take the hook,
or just nip the ends and swim away?
Or was the bobbing just a wave?
Waiting for the line to signal—a jerk,
a tug saying "You've got one!"—
the thrill of the chase, the glory of the catch.

We rolled our pants legs a turn or two
above the knee, and waded in
(our fathers used waders, but that was
grown-up dignity laughable on a kid)
sinking ankle-deep in the mud atop
the hard-pan bottom, wading back to the bank

with each fish, or to rebait,
or just to take a breather and pull
the bloodsuckers off our legs—
long summer twilights.
And I've gone after girls, in my time,
deep in the shit you have to spread,

baiting hooks, dropping lines,
stringing the catch, avoiding the stingers,
picking off leeches—
I have no tale of the big fish
that got away, but oh my god,
that one blonde. . .

Halloween

Yvonne, just a few lines,
this last day of October,
against the ghosts and goblins
of the falling year.

Last week a touch of frost,
catching a vineful of tomatoes,
the last dregs of the garden.
Just an hour ago I watched

the two houses across the street
notch the chrome-clouded sun,
the bird-bath catch molten gold,
and a wedge of geese returning

to the reservoir, the dusk
alive with their honkings.
I know you know how I thrive
on such manifestations;

you do too. But we can't escape
the witches—those old Celts & Druids
knew the seasons of the year
and the soul—that haven't changed.

I don't watch the horror shows
that populate TV these nights,
can't understand those who do.
I guess they don't wake in wee hour,

cold fingers pumping their hearts,
wordless presence prickling their pores.
Clemmie and I rattle in this house
that raised and sent forth five children,

her cello stands, locked in case,
my class notes moulder in manilla,
disuse, decay order our lives.
But on the dining table

two glasses of vin rosé
remind of summer grapes
and vines heavy with promise,
inform these lines I think and pen—

as May inheres in Halloween,
as setting sun portrays the dawn.
You and I use words, Vonnie,
and lines, to ground the ghosts—

day after day, spelling the night.

Cops and Robbers

We chased each other, shooting
with homemade rubber guns.
Rule was you had to drop dead,
if killed, count to fifty,
then resurrect, rejoin the fun.
Hit in the arm or leg
you were only wounded,
losing the use of the limb.
Worse than dying,
because you didn't recover.

"John Dillinger and his gang
just held up the bank in Mason City."
Rollie Considine, usually a captain,
burst on us with this bulletin.
"He's heading this way."

As one we all
(except Cry Baby Jimmy Nelson)
ran to the edge of town,
stretched out flat behind the railroad tracks
where we could look across the rails
and down on US 18.

"One of the gang was wounded,
and had to be helped into the car."
We waited for Dillinger and his gang,
coming west from Mason City,
half an hour away.
"Maybe they'll stop
and make ol' Doc Shaw
take the bullet out."
We savored that idea,
knowing it would really put our little town
in the news.
We were in the real world, now,
Though death was still a count of fifty,
and the sky was turning pink,
the air thick.
We were at the bottom of the bowl
in a strawberry ice-cream world,
waiting for John Dillinger.

Sunbathe

The Sunday morning sun pushing against
the south suburban window has already
lifted the curtain of early fog,
lapped the dew off the grass,
chased shadows down strewn alleys,
long country lanes. He is no
morning stroller taking a constitutional,
this exerciser, no runner
trimming his love handles.

He finds her in the breakfast nook,
licking the crumbs of toast and jelly
from her fingers, sipping coffee,
reading the world and nation's news.
He streams through her pane,
a golden shower, unperceived,
forms a square of light behind
her chair, climbs her back.
She arches, rubs—if a cat,
would be purring, kneading
a lap. His light, strong fingers
massage her strapless shoulders,
move up her neck, part her hair.
He kisses the nape, floods her
with his warmth,

is sated, moves on, up the street,
shining in every bedroom window,
exercising his seigneurial rights.
Meanwhile she, in bathroom now,
flushed, radiant, feels herself aglow,
a radiator pulsing warmth,
draws the shade, the shower curtain,
leans against even warmer fingers.

How to Grow Young Painting Pictures

First, quit abstracting.
Mind games are for old men
whose fingers spill the drink,
fumble the buttons.
Brush as if you held the turtle's deed
for four centuries, for finishing first.
Wear a one-handed watch.
Let your eye teach your hand.

Abandon glorious sunsets, turn east,
reverse the long cavalcade, clear
your pores in Roman baths, sketch
the hetaera's grace and bloom, turn
savage and social in bearskin, unselfish.
Be shaman blowing blue horses
on cave walls. One with your subject.
Let your heart teach your eye.

Put away your palette, your brushes,
forget the nudes, take up crayons.
Draw stick figures at play,
animals in flight. Make a hundred
preliminary studies, shade in the colors,
stray outside the lines—if lines there be.
Forget the rules,
grow simple and unstressed, primary.
Let your hand teach your heart.

Reconstruct the Harmonies

*And so we dance, this Indiana summer,
compose, reconstruct the harmonies —
twist and step, glide and dip . . .*

Somatic

Milk and Honey

I was first-born, and eight days late,
bottle fed white milk from white goats;
with tow forelock and dagwood cowlicks
crept and walked and ran; under straw hat
shading fair skin threshed oats and made hay
in simmering midwest sun; in white shirt
and striped tie ice-cream dated, kissing
her home under a silver moon.

College, fluorescent library, and
pale gold beer; white carnation slow dancing
books and girls and midnight bull
three subsidized GI years; then married,
with white-gold bands and white wine toasts,
a yellow-gold girl with emerald eyes.

Because It's There

With the insouciance of all
my twelve years, I climbed
the windmill's sixty feet,
the iron rungs sharp on my
callused insteps, gravity
and the grease pail tugging
at my belt. I was the sailor
swarming up the main mast
to furl the sails in a heavy sea,
I was Tarzan, Lord of the Jungle
racing on bare feet through
the leafy canopy, answering
a call for help.

Reaching the platform, I clung
with one hand to the wheel's shaft
and peered out over the barn's ridge,
down on the house's faded shingles.
I was level with the swaying tops
of trees, could see into bird nests
hidden from below. I felt the wind,
stronger up here, drying the sweat
along my arms and down my back,
lifting my straw hat. I was
King of the Air.

I looked north, east, south, west,
over the growing fields of green corn,
of oats just beginning their pale
into yellow, the mowed hay fields
putting out new shoots of second growth.
Could see the cows, black and white,
in the far pasture, look down the road
at neighbor, neighbor, tiny people,
and dogs, in the yards. Could see
Mrs. Hedlund hanging out her wash,
underwear on the inside line,
could see the mailman, five boxes away,
stopping at the Lokens. I was a spy,
a roving eye, seeing what was denied
earthbound mortals. I was loose, and free.

Purple Cow

Second grade, and in barefoot May
Miss Nelson gave the class
a picture to color
a grazing cow, grass, flowers
a sky and sun.

Blue, unclouded sky
round, yellow sun
green grass with red poppies
I left the cow till last
made it purple
soft, lilac strokes
carefully staying inside the lines.

A single cow, no other cow
not a bell cow, leading the herd
a not unhappy cow
purple, with white spots
grazing in the field.

I was Miss Nelson's favorite
and warmed in her approval
not really minding
the playground taunts, "teacher's pet"
but she refused my purple cow.
"Arthur, you know that's not right."

And gave me another picture.
I colored the cow all purple
ignoring the drawn-in spots.
Coming up the aisle, Miss Nelson gasped,
I grinned
and she kept me after school.

So there I sat
in my third-row seat
blank cow on my desk
staring at me.
Miss Nelson at the front
busy at her teacher's desk
the big wall clock ticking.

I took the worn-down crayon
peeled paper away
purpling my nail
and with dark, glossy strokes
layer on layer
savaged the cow
going outside the lines
a jagged, purple cow.

Which caused Miss Nelson
again to gasp
and this time her flying hand
slapped me, hard
as she never had, any kid.
We stared at each other,
dear Miss Nelson, somewhere

till you turned and ran
back to your desk
and head on arms
you sobbed
blonde curls trembling
like tall dandelions
pelted by spring shower.

Volunteers

Not a break in the skin anywhere.
No blood. But the engineer,
the trainmen knew. They fenced the corpse
with their living bodies, protective,
abashed by death. They looked
at each other like men who had failed,
seeing the dropped touchdown pass,
the washing out of pilot school,
the locked door. Down the track
the old Ford still clung
to the front of the engine.

The car's front door was sprung;
the man had landed fifteen feet away,
in tall grass and fragile blue flowers,
was curled as if asleep.
When the firemen arrived, small-town volunteers,
they handled him as if he might break,
as if something sharp inside
might come loose and poke through.
The chief later said he thought of
shattered windows in burning buildings
and being careful of the jagged edges.

One of the firemen tried to fit the billed cap
back on the man's head; dropped it
on his chest. "Look, he's fresh-shaved."
"Probably on the way to the funeral director,"
the town marshall said. "His wife died
this morning." The handlers all looked
in different directions. "Whom do we notify?"

"There's kids in school, five or six, so
the superintendent. The Reverend. Gus
for the body. Jerry Tweito, at the bank,
he's a fishing buddy. One of them'll know
a relative." The oldest son, brought home
from college by the mother's expected death,
was there alone when they brought him the news.
Nothing for him; his Uncle Martin, the Dad's brother,
had been located. The body, the car, the funerals
all were being arranged.

A new volunteer, back behind his
realtor's desk, picked stick-tites
from his trousers' leg.   It was his first body.
His leg, propped on the desk drawer,
would not stop shaking.

Last Words

What was my father thinking
in the last seconds
of his life?
Thecarbrakesfailingthetrainwhistling
at the crossing—

life-long ironist, was it appreciation,
dying
in perfect health?

grief, not caring,
because his liver-cancered wife
had died just that morning?

confusion, dying at fifty,
intestate, on the way
to arrange her funeral?

regret, guilt,
leaving six futures
upset, unsettled?

relief, that he had refused
my offer to go along
on this trip to the funeral parlor?

Forecast

September, frost whitecaps
the sea of grass beyond
the window. My cancered mother,
weatherproof in the rented
hospital bed, rouses,
as my sister, bringing Mom's
breakfast tray, says the day
will be sunny and warm.

As her sister and brothers,
gathered from afar,
husband, and children
one by one visit the room,
the rest of us drink coffee,
make small talk
in the living room.

Hanging in the common air,
nothing to do, but wait.

Gravity

On her death bed
my sweet unfinished mother
kissed me, the inner rot
of cancered liver on her breath.
She lingered two more days;
then Dad woke me, 4 A.M.
"She's gone." He crashed the car,
hours later, on the way
to make arrangements.
Died himself as young as she.
No good-bye to any of us.

A double funeral
in best Sunday suit
and dress. Later, carver's
error, engraved in stone
put Mom's death date
one year wrong,
one year later,
denying them
their final togetherness.
For fifty years
the rains of September
have reminded me
of God's memorial joke.

Genevieve Walrath Madson, 1896-1949

A night and most of a day, and still it snows,
a foot already, after a long warm fall,
the lawns staying green into solstice but now
accepting, open-armed, this white embrace
that shifts and drifts and turns the landscape
into something else. I wonder how this prairie
formed, and why I'm thinking sand and beach.
No boardwalks here, nor T-shirt stores
to crowd us into vacation acts.
Just the snow falling, falling, swirling,
blanketing the sleeping earth. It is
the first week of the New Year, and you are old
in the ground, and long away, as the world
snows, and I write this missive.

You, if you think at all, turn away
from winter, from the snow you hated,
even though Dad always did the shoveling,
turn to your other son basking
on San Pedro Coast, blue water, warm sand,
bare feet—summer thoughts. That in this
record snowfall I can pull the quilt around
my ears and walk the sand, is really something;
that I can stand and watch the prairie
fill with dreams, is something;
that I am remembering you as the snow
remembers its place in the great plan,
is a stopping of the heart,
is really something.

Genealogy

Entering Arlington, Iowa, the town
my mother's great-grandfather Isaac platted—
no sign pointing to a 'Business District,'
but after wandering just a bit, we find downtown—
a block and a half of sick, palsied,
buildings, bent with weather,
beaten with age. Boarded fronts, broken windows,
weed-cracked parking lots; two places only
showing some vigor, a side-by-side bar
and gift shop, whose shop-lady
sends us out of town, four miles
of narrow country road.

The cemetery is green, mowed, maintained.
A double strip of beige gravel leads from
the arched gate and doubles back,
splitting the green. Stone markers row neatly,
flowers pink and white. Even the faded memorials
in the old section stand up straight.
We find three separate ancestral plots,
my grandparents, Ble and Lizzie Genung Walrath,
his parents, Dan and Eliza Deming Walrath,
and the chiseled dates of Dan's father,
Black Hawk War fifer Isaac and his wife,
Caty Zoller Walrath, and assorted other Demings,
Genungs, and Brauns. Amy takes pictures,
her great-great-great grandparents.
We leave, bypassing Arlington.
We don't want to follow the ordered,
bordered territory of the dead
with the entropy of the dying.

Unendowed Chair

Receiving the chair, a captain's chair,
arms that half-surround, back
that fits the average professor's
curved spine, hitting just below
the blades, seat deep for padded
cushion (not included), no swivel,
no castors, sturdy wood, black,
university seal embossed in gold—
chair awarded for twenty-five years
professing, chair—a humorless joke
ceremoniously presented, the chancellor
smiling, I—polite, inwardly wry.

A captain's chair—captain of what?
Not a ship—this chair at sea?
Not of industry—not throne-like enough.
Not a chair to head a classroom,
teach from, not an office-chair
for the consulting student, nor
yet a chair to read in. An
impractical chair. The perfect symbol.

Genealogist
for Clemmie

You suspected arid results
and resisted the urge to dig.
Filled out a family tree,
names instead of ribbed leaves,
dates but no sun-sucking chlorophyll.
No personalities, no plots, no pictures,
just passenger lists, census rolls,
marriage registries—but wait, wait, here's
a Revolutionary Veteran's
Milford, Massachusetts, will, in which,
near the end, he lists the household wares,
including kitchen pots and pans,
three five-inch, two seven-inch, pewter,
and one seven-inch copper bottomed,
enumerates his wife's clothing, including
her underwear—seven petticoats, two
with lace ribbons, one pink, one blue,
as among his property—willing them to her.

What was the urge to know? What kept
you at the machine, scanning, scanning,
skipping lunch so as not to lose your place?
Now that it's summer and the tree shines
green and bushy, all filled out, do you say
to the father you barely knew, early gone,
there, there's your place; your father's
father, and his father, their places;
say to your mother, who was sixty years
of conflicts, who is still a congeries
of negative examples, but finally to be
pitied and forgiven, there, there's
your place, that twig on that branch.
By their places shall you know them.
And you, this is who you are, descended of.
And in your will, will you bequeath
something more than petticoats?
The green-thumbed woman who grew the tree?
Be sure to include the portrait made
for your senior recital, slim, blonde,
with already, behind the smile, silk-clothed steel.

Portrait

That Sarabande with golden glow
would overflow the practice room,
flood the whole house with exalting,
were not you and Bach so twinned.

Because of you, the cello
enthrones the glitter and glory
of heaven's promise. But only my ear
to rejoice, my eye to prize.

My pen scratches slowly, more lines
crossed out than saved. No word
or hopeless figure really catches
your transports, rhapsodies.

Base poet I, failing at portraiture;
paired souls, you and the suite.
Pictured grace eludes my fingers,
brain. A poem incomplete.

My mind holds only the room,
the glow, the music overspilling.
Still, in all this gold
I see, centered, you. You.

Elbows and Onions

I come home from work, in from the cold,
and there she is, wielding a knife,
slicing onions to garnish the broil,
dicing onions to spice the salad.
We eat onions because they're recommended,
and in self-defense, and it's like saving a life,
since my bypass and her gall bladder.

She's crying over those onions,
delicate and substantial, like a stew
she's simmered all day in the crock pot,
seasoned with basil, oregano, peppers,
and salt substitutes, these days—
perfuming herself. Her lips are puckered around
kitchen matches, giving them my kiss,
but her busy elbows promise,
under the peel, inside the rose, is treasure.

We hug in the kitchen, thighs and groins
caressing, elbows, hers bare, fitting palms
like plug in socket. Each is incandescent
for the other, round and firm,
like bulbs in the sack, in the stew,
on the plate, on the breath,
in a matchless kiss.

Tomatoes Are Ripe, Are Ripe

Frost tonight, the weatherman warned,
and so he picks green tomatoes,
those showing streaks of pink
of red, weighing their roundness,
feeling their curves fitting his palm
like the baseball of his playing days,
like the breast of the first girl
he'd unhooked.

Thirty now line his window ledges,
ripening in the autumn sun, all of them
candidates for perfection.
Some harvesters he knows, he's seen,
bite, eat the fruit like an apple,
holding, turning it in their hands,
juice running down their chins
like bleeding wounds. Some cooks,
he knows, he's seen, fry green tomatoes
like slices of liver in a pan.

He can't bear the thought of such
desecration. He paces the floor
in late afternoon, the sun fading,
composing a poem, trying to capture
ripeness, *redness*, remembering,
anticipation. Their curves and his
will intersect, he'll peel and slice,
season and swallow, and he will feel
the juice like spring rain in his brain,
the seeds will germinate in his veins,
and he will bleed all over the page.

Sumac

Clemmie knows a dozen banks
where sumac grows red,
first scarlet of the fall,
a month before the green has fled
the oak leaves.

We pick an August afternoon
and drive along County D
where redness fills the ditch,
more scarlet than the Judas Tree
on Easter Eves.

We break a branch, here and there,
not stripping any bush,
and carry home to give
our living room the flush
of red ripe berries.

And when the snow begins to blow,
and Christmas greens, and reds,
New Year's mistletoe
arrive, we'll put the sumac out
for chickadees.

Taking Off

Sitting on the runway, twenty minutes,
thirty minutes, delay, delay,
the snow swirling down, the flush
of dirty water down the windows
as they de-ice once again,
having second thoughts,
third thoughts.

They apologize for the wait,
serve juice, coffee,
our choice. The plane is warm,
bright, the motors hum, voices
hum, the stewardess squats
beside a girl in an aisle seat,
six, seven, traveling alone.

"It's like a womb," I say,
thinking *coffin* even as I speak,
seeing my father in his
in front of the church,
the file of viewers, the waxen skin,
cheeks rosed, eyes closed,
preserved, unnatural.

Clemmie and I fly together,
the kids grown, on their own,
and we have boarded
without any good-byes,
routine departure, just like my father,
driving off on the way
to his fatal crash.
And Clemmie's hand, seeking reassurance,
clutches mine.

Somatic

I recompose the girl you were,
Key of G, waltz time, the steps
of a dance and its whirl—
the warm gossip giggle summer laugh
of you, like the scarlet skip
of a row of tulips.

Arthritis glues the joints of your
music—the next tune's lament,
muffled drums, dead march—
but today, today, it's remission.

High noon, mid-summer, claret roses,
this respite like your cousin's wedding
dance, you played six hours,
or like the flowers you willed
to bloom, summer before last,
blossoms free of rust.

And so we dance, this Indian summer,
compose, reconstruct the harmonies—
twirl and step, glide and dip,
moonshine as festive as Strauss.

Snow

"No two are a pair," Clemmie says,
watching through our picture window
as the snowflakes swirl down,
smoothing the yards into
a made bed.

I remember an art poster display
of twenty-four geometric shapes,
dazzling, intricate, symmetrical,
four white rows, like stars awarded
for perfect lessons,

and wonder by what formula
scientists know no two a pair.
I sink my sock-warm toes
into the rug, wind my arm
around her waist.

Winter and years squeeze us indoors,
all that singularity compacted
into one cozy blanket
stretching from the horizon
to here.

Snow men. Snow caves. Making rings
for fox and goose. Memories
crowd in like kisses
on a doorstep. Each one
unique.

"That was the year . . . we wrapped doors
in Christmas paper . . . we invented
un-birthdays . . . we crashed the car . . .
the second in Wisconsin . . .
wasn't it?"

Around the world a blizzard
of distinctions makes contradictions
of us all. Parents, grandparents,
we believe in snow flakes,
and snow balls, too.

The Next Degree

Each alumni news another classmate
has slipped over the page's edge, undertaken
the last assignment.

Winter's snows pile higher, longer,
too many beds are newly single,
and thaws are briefer.

Clemmie and I await the spring,
subscribe to mags, read the stories,
fend vicissitude.

We study the books,
sit up nights,
all-night sessions, cramming for
the last exam.

Monet's Haystacks

They sit so confidently in the sun
and shadows, side by side
amid the slopes, our eyes
slide inward, and we know
secrets. Follow the coarse grass
down into the darkness where
the humans who built these stacks
must house, certainly not on these
bright uplands.

Haying weather now, Clemmie no longer
circling the date on the calendar,
sings more than she sighs.
I bought her, our first year,
a stuffed animal, green and yellow rabbit,
her first. Gifts had always been practical:
money, school shoes, party dresses,
piano lessons.

Today she likes blouses, sweaters—
flowers. Looking at her in these presents,
sunlight smiling, like Monet I paint
haystacks.

Invocation

I settle in my recliner,
contemplate the shelves,
books turning their backs,
the stack of paper waiting
to be filed, as if that were
an answer, the desk piled
with fat folders, shadows
growing in their corners.

I claim them all; they're nothing,
everything. In the kitchen Clemmie
stirs the pot that keeps us
warm and fed.

I correspond with the banked fires,
trading epilogs; I want to write like a man
whose nose has inhaled the flower,
whose hands have dug at roots,
whose heart's a bobbing log in
the red mill race beneath his skin.

And I think
of an orchestra scraping, tuning,
shifting in their seats
for the winter season's final concert—
let me be the maestro.

Let the harmonies that rise
from my strings and horns
be a symphony to raise the roof
shored above our heads.

Let everyone, on stage
and out front, make
glorious music, all together.
Be a band of angels.
Sing Hallelujah.

Witching the Night

"Gray suit," I mutter, looking at my sleeve,
then smile, force the chuckle
prescribed for stress.
What color, really, is hard to say,
the suit's so thatched with thread-wide stripes
and slanting lines, between—brown, I think,
and half of them blue—or green?
Myopia blurs.
"Green suit," you always say,
as this morning, bringing it when I called
from the bathroom.

I sit up half the night, these days,
late movie, late book—
I'd only toss in bed—
while you're a daytime person,
early to bed and turnless sleep,
up early refreshed—I rouse
at your bounce, we're husband and wife,
and then I drowse
till ten,
or noon.

You blue your eyes,
green your eyes,
gray your eyes
by the top you wear,
your hair blonde, whatever blouse,
pale as youth, still blonde.

In the sun, in the shade, down the malls
your gray, green, blue eyes
sing, smile, brighten for me,
laugh, gleam, lighten for me,
hold back the walls.

Asleep in bed,
you're still up late with me,
starring in the movie,
illustrating my books.
Your curls beckon, bounce for me,
pledge, plume, flounce for me,
witch the darkening night,

and I plait for you,
gray-green poems,
slant-thatch lines.

White Wine

Another day, like most, unmemorable.
Mid-morning, my brother called, not bad news,
just on a whim, and we talked politics
and the weather. The rest of the morning
we read, Clemmie a mystery, I a thriller,
haloed under our separate lamps.
We lunched healthily, on broccoli soup.
Then I to my study, and revising,
the kind of work that never relents,
that ever renews. Re-joined Clemmie
at the kitchen table for a glass
of Zinfandel, watching finches at the feeder
flash their colors, crowding, cramming.
When the high point of your day, as far as
event, is the arrival of the mail,
you know you're living peace and contentment,
though no excitement, except the unplanned kiss
as we bump, re-capping the wine.
A nap or doze before dinner, and then,
as the smell of ready-for-the-stove
Chicken Kiev wafts from the oven,
I chop celery and onion for the salad,
sparing my fingers and thumb, and Clemmie
sets the table. We finish the meal,
no leftovers to refrigerate, and settle
into the evening routine, puzzle
and program, book and pencil,
go to bed knowing a graceful day,
a solstice present, a day that unfolded
like a lacquered fan, and turn out the lights,
inviting dreams to order the night.

Closets

The annual church drive
for used clothing, and Clemmie
is after me to weed my closet.
"You have jackets twenty years
out of style, sweaters
getting holes on the shelf,
five shirts still store-cellophaned."

"Give the older things away
while they're still of use,"
she says, and "We need the space."
We used to share a closet,
but since the kids left,
we each have our own.
I haven't bought anything that hangs
since I retired, and it looks
like I won't as long as Christmas
and Father's Day stick in the calendar.

So I don't wear the jackets,
don't wear out the shirts,
and they grow shabby enough
for the homeless. But they're flowers,
not weeds; it hurts even to think
uproot. They make my winter summer.

Our son, six inches taller,
and colored like his mother,
can't wear them. Someday
Clemmie can take them
to the church, along with me,
and then there'll be lots of space.
It's a lingering, piecemeal going
I resist.

The Man Who Lived Among the Cannibals

Re-reading Melville, I jump ship with him,
go native, re-fresh, grow youthful again,
stong in joint and sinew, in resolve.
I crib notes in my palm, curl my fist
on *Typee, Tahiti,*
watch brown-skinned girls
plait white flowers in their hair.
The West Wind unclothes me;
it carries blue lagoons in its bosom,
smells of red lianas. Shall I wear
a lei around my neck, eat papayas?

Perhaps I should close the book on Herman,
on youth. A few chapters of *Typee* bring
the serpent of western civ, of Christian
missionaries poisoning Paradise.
Like a vampire, I see no one in the mirror,
see the wall over my shoulder, closing in.
I remember the WPA outdoor pool,
remember firm bodies in stretch-wool
swimming suits, water and sun and sand.

Today, aging, retired, memory-driven,
the words of the book beginning to swim,
I put it down, retreat into summer softball
on the school playground, Luther League
social hour, the walk home through safe,
dark streets, the door-step kiss.
Eternally surprised at how it
comes back, every year more, not less.
The scenes accrete, enrich.

It is not Melville's fault, who quit
the Pacific twice, in life, in books,
turned east. If I get nostalgic,
it is a disease of flesh, not spirit.
Like that boy attending catechism
because of the girls, spouting paganisms
to draw their concern. Meanwhile, I don't
foreclose tomorrow; sailing east
to the South Pacific is passing through
Sunda Straits to white sands, and calm shores.

Visitation

The sheets a tangle,
the back-gapped gown a bunch.
He twists and turns as much
as he can, tethered to the many-branched
IV tree, no position really
comfortable—just as he has lived,
seventy-odd years, a sore finger
others are always bandaging,
others are always explaining.

He claimed his middle L
stood for Lucifer, which all ignored,
nobody believed, least of all
his Clemmie. He asks now
about the bills, have they been paid.
"Yes, yes," she says, too quickly,
but he does not push.
He's fighting to stay alive,
to remain relevant. Clemmie
helps him rise from the bed,
wincing at his gasp. "Lean on me,"
she says, trying to make her strength
something other than an offense.

Intensive Care

The world lurched,
the sun winked,
and I saw myself from above
stretched on a table
surrounded by a fence of green gowns,
the room suffused
from an incandescent bloom
high on the stem of one wall—
seven hours, they later said,
one tick, it seemed.
A foretaste of eternity.

But I am anguished this morning,
stapled and tube-connected,
thinking of mortality,
thinking of the girls and women
who slowed time,
who have gone forward
in their together lives,
distancing me.

I would love one to step backward—
wafting a cologne
the essence of seventeen,
of the bliss of first abandon,
or thirty-eight, with manhattans
on her breath, and the biological clock
on her mind, or fifty-three,
graying around the edges
but tender in the center—
and join me in
irritating the oyster.

I imagine
an inspired she-and-I
inventing together
a memory that never happened,
worthy of pearling.
We would be stop-framed,
movie stills in poster colors,
lip-synced Hollywood stars.
I foretaste sweet eternity.

Facing Forward

Yesterday we set out flowers,
perennials, filling in, thickening
the front-yard beds, annual project,
the last three years, since you retired.
You straightened, stood, hand caressing
the crick in your back, green shirt,
red cap, listening to the house finch
in the apple tree. Together we
looked ahead, reaped summer colors,
gathered fall bouquets.

Today, shut inside by May thunder,
my hand grips a pencil, scrawls
words across a page. I rub
the new callus beneath
the white-gold band, ring which
fits more neatly each blossoming
year. I sip my coffee, listen
to the finch, see the larkspurs,
picture words, as the rain patters.

So many gifts, over the years,
and on Mother's Day, the best,
you—in green shirt, red cap,
straightening against the rolling years.

Golden Year

I wanted to share today's walk
with you—my heart repaired, the grass green,
the tulips a red and yellow laugh
in the south wind, the light and shadow
from maple and ash painterly
on lawn and walk.

I wanted you along, a pheromonal sweat
in the crisp, fresh, newly warm air,
to be outside together, expanding—
the indoors we breathed all those months
suddenly a prison, the enforced closeness
an invasion.

I wanted you around the neighborhood,
but your arthritis doesn't permit
perambulation—so it's the sun and I,
the warmth on my back, the cautious
promise of another April, and then home
to your improbable touch.

Assent, and Bright Lights

A wounded heart walks the mall,
where bright lamps cast no shadows.
His calves tire, breath grows short,
but he is content; he's almost
on schedule, nine laps in the hour,
and he can rationalize the slowness
by the crowds clogging the pathways.
He compares himself to shoppers
he overtakes, women bulging their slacks
and shirts, men with paunches
and fat shoulders. Good;
never mind the other walkers,
arms pumping, who lap him.
He has persevered, finished the hour,
will not be disappointed
meeting his wife for the ride home.

I want to tell Clemmie about the contentment,
define myself, say something about
the lack of shadows, but the words
don't come, and she is busy, driving.

After Shock

We were broadsided
in the intersection
other guy ran a red light
though I had thought
but didn't say
you were going a little fast.
We all walked away but both cars killed,
and then I collapsed.

You rode with me holding my hand
paramedics saying
"Fine you're going to be fine"
waking up feeling the knife
no longer there.
No one can say why the heart attacks,
you gave mine regular doses
of close attention—
oh serpent's truth.

Suppose the jumper cables
hadn't worked
hadn't kicked my pump
back in gear
and my closed-eye poems
died with me on the table.
I have to believe
it would have made
no difference at all.

After the Bypass

Children, you will call,
and I could talk a little
of the pain, of how it feels
to be a horizon stretched
from edge to edge,
of pills that eat the night
but leave the knife undigested,
of how, from inside my sheeted cage
the shine, the configuration
of fixed stars flicker
like bulbs burning out.

But I'd rather, with pencil on paper,
tell you of my good luck—
a heart that still leaps
when the image nestles down,
a heart that warms
when figures seem pointed
as a new moon,
as children making it on their own.
So what if my feet won't skip,
and I thin to a line.
Waxing moons must wane.

Children, here for your eyes,
for your arms and hearts—
I've seen the words you wish we'd spoken,
burning in the sky.
See how they warm, move,
last.

Evening at Home

The eye that closes at dusk
winks a dark conspiracy. You reach

through the hanging between us. The russet
mums beside the front stoop gather

the fading light tenderly, like a worn wallet
molded to fit a hip, a granddaughter's

portrait in cellophane. Like creeping shadows,
yellow maple leaves descend the steps.

Look how the stem and lobes drift
and curl inward, curl like fingers closing

in a grasp. How do we know the season
enhances us? We touch lips, essences.

The rusty mums lose their color in
the purple pulse of evening. Clemmie,

we are the flowers' stained petals blooming
toward a frost we cannot predict, cannot stay.

Trumpet

Everyone knows the story about
Gabriel's trumpet—Earth's last breath
expended through the tubes and bell
and sounding again the note the shepherds
heard that night, in the hills;
sounding the flourish scholiasts heard
as Music of the Spheres;
and the dead in all their vaults
and urns and scattered ashes
thrill at the signal, snap
their finger bones,
buck and wing.

And all God's creatures
release the songs locked up inside them:
the mocked mouse and silent swan,
cicada grub in its fifteenth year,
mammoth frozen whole in the ice,
join in the Hallelujah Chorus,
and the orchestra, forests, of course,
the woodwinds, the rocks and mountains
and treeless plains the tympany, the rivers
and lakes the strings, following
the Conductor's beat.

But it's the color I anticipate,
the color of the end, the color
of the spheres, the whole umbrella sky
a rainbow band of seven times seven
colors; every thread of every leaf
and fur and fiber iridescent with
new astounding colors;
every soprano voice exploding
in yellows beyond yellow,
red tenors and green contraltos
and the rich dark browns of bass—
ultra-reds and infra-blues—
the voice made visible,
and we vibrate, tune to the One Fork,
become a symphony of color—
oh, eyes at last that see.

Raised on an Iowa farm, Arthur Madson described himself as 'a lapsed agrarian.' Yet his farming childhood lives on in his poems, and his love of gardening stayed with him over the decades. Born in June 1925, Arthur lived until April 2008. At his memorial service his family celebrated him as husband, father, grandfather, big brother, uncle, teacher, storyteller, poet and scholar. His fellow poets saw him as quick-witted, wry, and unmatched in his nuanced portrayal of fellow humans. Humor was a mainstay for him, and he used it artfully, both on the page and at the podium.

Arthur enjoyed a long marriage to cellist Marianne McDaniel Madson, the beloved 'Clemmie' in his poems. Over the years, the partners, who had been college sweethearts, encouraged each other's creativity and raised five children together. Arthur served in the army during World War II and afterward earned his PhD at the University of Oklahoma. He began writing in his mid-fifties and joined the Wisconsin Fellowship of Poets after reading his poems at the Wisconsin State Capitol on Poetry Day. He served as vice president of WFOP and editor of its annual poets' calendar.

He taught English for thirty-six years, most of them at the University of Wisconsin-Whitewater. A Shakespeare scholar who was also versed in the works of Melville and other literary greats, he delighted students and other audiences with his insightful lectures. He joined a biweekly manuscript group in Madison and began publishing soon afterward. His work appeared in many magazines and four books—*Good Manure, Blue-Eyed Boy, Plastering the Cracks* and *Coming Up Sequined*.